CHRIST ABOVE ALL

THE BOOK OF HEBREWS

Other titles in the Transformative Word series:

The Universal Story: Genesis 1–11
by Dru Johnson

Deserting the King: The Book of Judges
by David Beldman

Finding God in the Margins: The Book of Ruth
by Carolyn Custis James

Glimpsing the Mystery: The Book of Daniel
by Barbara M. Leung Lai

God Behind the Scenes: The Book of Esther
by Wayne K. Barkhuizen

When You Want to Yell at God: The Book of Job
by Craig G. Bartholomew

Faith Amid the Ruins: The Book of Habakkuk
by Heath A. Thomas

Revealing the Heart of Prayer: The Gospel of Luke
by Craig G. Bartholomew

Together for the World: The Book of Acts
by Michael R. Wagenman

Cutting Ties with Darkness: 2 Corinthians
by John D. Barry

Living Doctrine: The Book of Titus
by Daniel L. Akin

Between the Cross and the Throne: The Book of Revelation
by Matthew Y. Emerson

CHRIST ABOVE ALL

THE BOOK OF HEBREWS

TRANSFORMATIVE WORD

ADRIO KÖNIG

Series Editors
Craig G. Bartholomew & David Beldman

LEXHAM PRESS

Christ Above All: The Book of Hebrews
Transformative Word

Lexham Press, 1313 Commercial St., Bellingham, WA 98225
LexhamPress.com

Print ISBN 9781683592853
Digital ISBN 9781683592860

Series Editors: Craig G. Bartholomew and David Beldman
Lexham Editorial: Abby Salinger, Abigail Stocker, Holly Marr
Cover Design: Brittany Schrock
Typesetting: Abigail Stocker

TABLE OF CONTENTS

FOREWORD

What a privilege to participate in this series! I am a 79-year-old, white, middle-class, privileged, male South African. I was born in the high days of apartheid and feel a resemblance to Paul, who wrote that he was "born at the wrong time" (1 Cor 15:8 NLT). From my childhood onward, I could never accept the way blacks were treated in South Africa—not for political reasons but for religious ones. I simply could not relate it to the love of Jesus.

I grew up in the evangelical holiness movement, studied Christian philosophy and Reformed theology, was heavily influenced by the great German theologian Karl Barth, and slowly moved from systematic theology to biblical theology and exegesis. In this volume I am interested not only in the direct meaning of the text but also in the broader context and meaning in terms of the biblical message as a whole and in doctrinal issues.

INTRODUCTION: THE MAIN THEMES IN HEBREWS

Some think that the Letter to the Hebrews is the most neglected of all the New Testament writings. Why? Is it because it is so different from all the other letters? Even the great German Reformer Martin Luther had doubts about the canonicity of Hebrews.

Several issues make Hebrews a challenge to interpret. Firstly, we do not know who wrote this letter; most modern scholars reject the ancient view that it was by Paul,[1] although the mention of "our brother Timothy" in Hebrews 13:23 indicates that the recipients of the letter were associated with the apostle Paul and his circle. We do not know to which community the letter was written, and its date can only be positioned somewhere between AD 50–90.[2] Luke, of the Gospel of Luke and the Acts of the Apostles, and Apollos have been proposed as authors, but we cannot be sure who wrote Hebrews. Cockerill notes:

> The description of Apollos in Acts 18:24–19:1 is a description of the kind of person who

wrote Hebrews. The superior education of the writer of Hebrews is evident from his rhetorical skill. Its writer was steeped in Scripture and a competent expositor of its meaning, just as was Apollos. The book of Hebrews is the work of a powerful preacher with a deep pastoral concern for his hearers. Apollos's skill in demonstrating Christ's messiahship from the OT is in accord with the pastor's Christological exposition. Apollos's ability to confound Jews who did not acknowledge Christ fits well with the apparent Jewish-Christian elements in the recipients' background.[3]

Secondly, Hebrews not only refers more often to the Old Testament than any other New Testament book, but it includes alarmingly negative views of the Old Testament. One sometimes feels it is rejecting the Old Testament (e.g., chapter 10), a heresy that Marcion fell into in the time of the early church. But then it can also be so surprisingly positive about the Old Testament (Heb 11)!

MARCION

Marcion (c. AD 85–c. 160) was an influential figure in the early church whose teaching was eventually denounced. He drew a sharp distinction between the God of the New Testament and Yahweh of the Old Testament and rejected the Old Testament as non-Christian.

Thirdly, together with Galatians, it has the gravest warnings to believers about losing out on salvation—six in total. Believers can, therefore, find Hebrews a very disturbing letter to read.

We will come to these tough issues, but I encourage the reader not to be discouraged from diving into this book. In the foreword, I referred to how important the love of Jesus was in enabling me to see that the racism of apartheid was unacceptable. At the heart of Hebrews is a magnificent view of Jesus, a view that you do not want to miss out on.

Let us run through this letter to get a sense of just how exciting and relevant its message is for today.

OUTLINE OF HEBREWS[4]

I.   The Finality of God's Word in the Son (1:1–2:18)

II. The True Home of God's People (3:1–4:13)

III. The High Priesthood of Jesus (4:14–6:20)

IV. The Order of Melchizedek (7:1–28)

V.   Covenant, Sanctuary, and Sacrifice (8:1–10:18)

VI. A Call to Faith and Perseverance (10:19–12:29)

VII. Concluding Exhortation, Prayer, and Postscript (13:1–25)

Overview

We do not know who wrote Hebrews. However, from this letter, we can work out the state of its recipients.[5] The "Hebrews" had come to faith in Christ, but as they discovered just how hard the Christian life can be, they were tempted to fall back into the Judaism from which they had come to faith in Christ. They needed to be reminded again who Jesus is. Hebrews sets out to confront them again and again with the magnificent Christ.

Thus, although Hebrews makes for relatively easy reading, it has an urgent message. The main thrust of the message is clear. Simply page through this letter, and chapter after chapter, you will see the main theme for yourself: "Christ is greater than … ."

- Chapter 1: Christ is greater than the angels (1:4).

- Chapter 3: Christ is greater than Moses (3:3–6).

- Chapter 4: Christ is greater than Joshua and the rest that came through him (4:8–11).

- Chapter 7: Christ is greater than the priests (7:23–25).

- Chapter 8: Christ brings a better covenant (8:6, 7, 13).

- Chapters 8, 9: Christ offers his sacrifice in a bigger sanctuary (8:2; 9:11, 24).

- Chapters 9, 10: Christ offers a *bigger* sacrifice (9:11–14; 10:9–12).

In the context of this remarkable emphasis on the magnificence of Christ, the following themes come to the fore.

The Humanity and Humility of Christ

When you think of greatness, what comes to mind? We tend to associate magnificence with power, wealth, and authority, but, remarkably, in Hebrews we find the most emphatic emphasis in the entire New Testament on Christ's humility, his humanity, his being equal to us (2:10, 14–18; 4:15–16; 5:7–10).

The Use of the Old Testament

Not surprisingly in light of the readers' Jewish background, the Old Testament plays a major role in Hebrews. Hebrews is full of references and allusions to the Old Testament, and its use of the Old Testament is central to its structure.[6] So prevalent is the Old Testament in Hebrews that scholars are unclear how many quotations and allusions there are: numbers of quotations range from thirty-eight to twenty-nine.[7] Some twenty of the passages quoted are not cited elsewhere in the New Testament. Hebrews draws heavily on the Pentateuch and the Psalms, "the fundamental Law and the Book of common devotion," as Westcott describes them.[8] Psalms is the author's primary source for Christology, especially Psalm 110:1, 4.[9] Throughout the letter, the author uses the early Greek translation of the Old Testament, the Septuagint.

George Caird has proposed that Hebrews's argument is arranged around four Old Testament texts: Psalm 110:1–4; Psalm 8:4–6; Psalm 95:7–11; and Jeremiah 31:31–34. In each section after the first, the main quote is placed at the beginning. These texts make the case for the ineffectiveness of the Old Testament institutions, and other scriptural references supplement these four. Caird's creative theory did have a weakness: how to account for the exhortation in 10:19–13:21, which is integral to the structure of the letter. However, J. Walters developed Caird's theory, suggesting that the author of Hebrews arranged his argument in a series of six scriptural explications (illustrations), each framed with exhortation. He added Habakkuk 2:3–4[10] and Proverbs 3:11–12 to Caird's four passages.[11]

Caird's work has illuminated the way the author of Hebrews interpreted the Old Testament. Rather than the exegesis being allegorical and fanciful, it was "one of the earliest and most successful attempts to define the relationship between the Old and the New Testaments, and that a large part of the value of the book is to be found in the method of exegesis which was formerly dismissed with contempt."[12] The author is alert to the diversity in the Old Testament (Heb 1:1) but clearly sees the *same* God at work there as the one who has now spoken in his Son (Jesus). The author clearly embraces a theology of *fulfillment*, although he does not use the word.[13] Jesus fulfills and goes beyond the Old Testament.

The Six Warnings

The readers are in imminent danger of losing their faith in Jesus, and, as a result, a major feature of Hebrews is the repeated warnings, six in total. These are very serious admonitions, the most pressing ones in the entire New Testament (2:1–4; 3:1–4:13; 5:11–6:20; 10:26–39; 12:14–17; 12:25–29). It is clear that they relate directly to the main issue: the greatness of Christ. Letting go of Christ means losing out on everything.

The Calls to Persevere

Almost as urgent as these warnings are the calls to persevere. It is obvious that the author fears that the readers may opt out of the faith and turn their backs on Christ

(2:1–3; 3:12–14; 4:11, 14; 5:11; 6:1–3, 11–12; 10:22–25, 35–36; 12:1–3, 12, 25; 13:9). But on the other hand, even some of these calls contain assurances that the readers will persevere (6:9–10; 10:39).

SUGGESTED READING

☐ Using the outline of Hebrews above, browse through the letter as a whole, trying to get a sense of the major sections.

☐ Once you have done that, look up the verses connected to each of the main emphases. How do these verses emphasize those themes?

Reflection

Is it possible to have too small a view of Jesus? Why do you think this is the case?

_____

_____

_____

_____

How would you remind a friend thinking of giving up his or her faith of the magnificence of Christ? How does Hebrews do this for its readers?

_____

_____

_____

_____

As you begin your study of Hebrews, take some time to be still and pray that the Spirit would open you up again to the magnificence of Jesus. Spend some time worshiping him!

2

THE MAGNIFICENCE OF CHRIST IN A NUTSHELL

Nowadays, if we receive an email or a letter, we tend to ignore the introduction and leap to the substance of the message. However, in the world in which Hebrews was written, the introduction to a letter was really important: it often summarized the message in the opening lines (see, for example, Rom 1:1-6). This is especially true in long letters like Romans and Hebrews. Indeed, there is discussion among scholars about whether Hebrews really is a letter. Much of it seems more like a long sermon, and it is probably best to conclude that it is a sermon turned into a letter! However we resolve this issue, the introduction is crucial; in 1:1-4, the author summarizes his message about Jesus, and we will do well to pay close attention to these opening verses. They are full of rich teaching about Jesus:

> In the past God spoke to our ancestors through the prophets at many times and in various ways, but in these last days he has spoken to us by his Son, whom he appointed

heir of all things, and through whom also he made the universe. The Son is the radiance of God's glory and the exact representation of his being, sustaining all things by his powerful word. After he had provided purification for sins, he sat down at the right hand of the Majesty in heaven. So he became as much superior to the angels as the name he has inherited is superior to theirs. (Heb 1:1–4)

The first three verses are fundamental to the entire letter. In piling up descriptions of Christ, these three verses do two things:

- They summarize the essential message: the incomparable greatness of Christ.

- Like a hymn, they proclaim the matchless superiority of Christ.

Only John 1:1–3 and Philippians 2:6 come close to these verses in their evocation of the magnificence of Christ. Hebrews 1:1–3 is like Blackwell's bookstore in Oxford, England. From the outside, the store looks quite small, but once you go inside and start to explore, you discover that the store gets bigger and bigger, with multiple levels and huge rooms packed with books. If you read through these verses slowly, you will see that they tell us the following truths about Christ:

1. Through Christ, God spoke his final word: Christ is the final revelation of God.

2. Through Christ, God created the world: Christ is co-creator with God.

3. God appointed Christ heir of all things: Christ rules over everything.

4. Christ reflects the glory of God: he shares God's divinity.

5. Christ bears the very stamp of God's nature: he shares God's divinity.

6. Christ sustains all things by his powerful word: he holds our world in existence and cares for all things.

7. Christ provided purification from sin: he reconciled us to God.

8. Christ sits now at the right hand of the divine Majesty: Jesus is king!

Jesus is far bigger than we imagine, and these verses right at the beginning invite us to explore his magnificence.

Christ Is Greater than the Prophets (1:1–2)

We can only get to know God if he reveals himself to us. He has certainly done that in the Old Testament, but over against all the prophets of the Old Testament stands Christ as God's final and fullest revelation of himself.

The author of Hebrews starts with two ways in which God has spoken in history: the prophets and his Son. "Prophets" is the author's word for the whole of the Old Testament; in each case *God* spoke. The difference between the two ways is therefore not in the *one* who spoke but in the *medium* through which he spoke. His speaking through the Son is simply on a different level. It is one thing to send messengers with your message; it is another thing to come yourself. This is precisely what God did in Jesus. And it is in the "last days" or "the final days" (1:2 NJB) that he spoke through the Son. This means that God's Word, Jesus, is his final word. Never again will there come new words that are greater or richer than those through the Son. What we have in the New Testament is the full and final revelation of God prior to the return of Christ and the completion of history. Any new message or fresh word we receive from God will fit in with the words of Christ and the apostles he has appointed (see Acts 20:27; Col 2:2, 3, 9). Essentially, in the New Testament, we have the authoritative testimony of the apostles to Jesus so that any claim to be a word from God must always be tested against God's final word in Jesus.

Christ as Co-Creator (1:2)

J. B. Phillips wrote a provocative book entitled *Your God Is Too Small.* Alas, we are always in danger of having too small a view of Jesus. Hebrews explodes any such view. Jesus is not only God's *final* word but also his *first* word! He is Omega and Alpha! God created the world through Christ. Both John and Paul testify to the same truth (John 1:1–3; Col 1:15). So Christ really is the Alpha and the Omega, the beginning and the end, the first and the last (Rev 22:13).

Christ as the Heir of All Things (1:2)

Christ being co-creator of all things should leave us unsurprised that he also is the heir of all. This fits in with

Ephesians 1:10: God will unite all things under one head, Christ. One of the ways in which we diminish our view of Christ is by thinking that he came *only* to save our souls. He certainly did this, but as the creator and heir of all things, Christ came for a far greater work of redemption than just our souls: he is the redeemer and ruler of the whole creation. This means that we are called to serve and honor him in all areas of life as he has made it. However, Christ being the final word from God, the co-creator, and the heir of all things is still only the introduction. The climax is to come—in Hebrews 1:3.

Climax: Hebrews 1:3

Christ Is the Radiance of God's Glory and the Exact Representation of His Being

Here we have the most glorious words about Christ in the entire New Testament. He reflects the glory of God and "is the exact likeness of God's own being" (GNT). Only a few other words in the New Testament are comparable to these—for instance, "I and the Father are one" (John 10:30); "Anyone who has seen me has seen the Father" (John 14:9); and "in Christ all the fullness of the Deity lives in bodily form" (Col 2:9). Christ is in unity with and reflects God the Father in a unique way. He is *the* revelation of God. He is incomparable to anyone else.

It is worthwhile to take some time to unpack the meaning of these two statements more fully.

- Christ is the radiance of God's glory.
- Christ is the exact representation of God's being.

The two lines say the same thing, but the second line interprets and strengthens the first. God's "glory" and his "being" both refer to God himself, the essence of God, not merely something *about* God. In Christ, God's "radiance" and "exact representation," we meet God himself. "Radiance" implies "casting forth" what he receives. God's glory shines forth, and Christ catches this glory and reflects it, shines it forth to us. "Exact representation" then implies that Christ does not reflect something that he does not have in himself, something he only receives from outside; rather, he shines forth what he is in himself: God's glory, God himself. Nothing is to be "added" to Christ to get to God. He is God in his essence.

The Judeo-Christian view of God and the world rightly recognizes that God is radically different from us. He is God! He dwells in unapproachable light. Our greatest need is to know him, but we cannot do that on our own initiative. Imagine, for example, if you decided you wanted to get to know Queen Elizabeth as a friend. You could write to the palace; you could go to the palace. However, the only way you could get to know her is if she took the initiative and invited you to visit her. How much more so is this true of God. We can only get to know him if he takes the initiative—and Hebrews 1:1–3 tells us that he has done precisely this in Christ. As John 1:18 says, "No one has ever seen God. It is God the only Son, who is close to the Father's heart, who has made him known" (NRSV).

Christ Sustains All Things by His Powerful Word

This is not about who Christ is but about what he does. However, it confirms what has just been written about who he is. We know that providence—God's sovereignty over his entire creation—is ascribed to God himself. Now Christ is said to sustain everything. The New Testament, John in particular, emphasizes that Christ does what God does (John 5:19-21, 26).

But there is more in here than Christ merely carrying the world like Atlas as a weight on his shoulders. The CEV reads, "He holds the universe together" (Heb 1:3). He prevents the world from falling apart. The Old Testament describes God carrying—caring for and keeping safe—his people (Isa 46:4). The author of Hebrews has this Old Testament meaning in mind—except that here, it relates to the whole of the creation. That old chorus "he's got the whole world in his hands" is, in fact, true!

Christ "Has Provided Purification for Sins"

There is no way to speak about Christ without referring to reconciliation. He is our peace with God; through his blood we have redemption. We were reconciled to God through Christ's death; we were justified by his blood. Indeed, God has reconciled not just us but the world through Christ to himself (Eph 1:7; 2:14; Rom 5:8, 10; 2 Cor 5:19). Christ's work of redemption extends "as far as the curse (of sin and judgment) is found."[14] Through this reference to reconciliation, we are introduced to one of the central themes of Hebrews: the work of Christ as our high priest, not merely *bringing* the sacrifice but himself *being* the sacrifice for our sins (chapter 9-10).

He Sat Down at the Right Hand of the Majesty in Heaven

"The right hand of Majesty" is not only an indication of place but also of position, of authority. There is no one but Christ at God's right hand. Christ is unique. His authority is absolute. No one and nothing is comparable to him.

The Doctrine of the Trinity (1:1-3)

Hebrews 1:1-3 has much to teach us—not just about Jesus but about God. It is in such verses that we find the raw data that compelled the early church to formulate their understanding of God as the Trinity: one God in three persons. This is a mysterious doctrine, but it emerges clearly in passages like Hebrews 1:1-3.

Many criticize the view that God is a Trinity, one essence in three persons: Father, Son, and Holy Spirit. The criticism is directed more specifically at the divinity of Christ, that Christ is equal to God. Some claim that Jesus was an ordinary human being—a rabbi, a prophet, or a wisdom teacher—and that after his death believers "inflated" him: because they honored him, they tried to convince others to believe in him. But if we believe in the trustworthiness of the Bible, we can trust its emphasis on Christ's divinity, particularly in Paul's letters, John, and Hebrews.

In these writings the testimony comes through clearly and strongly that Jesus is the Christ, the Messiah, the Son of God, the revelation and even the presence of God, being equal to God, showing forth the glory of God, being the exact likeness of God, the one in whom the fullness of God dwells, the one through whom the Father himself is with us (Heb 1:3; John 5:18; 14:9; Col 2:9). Often, Christ himself is called God (John 1:1, 18; Rom 9:5; Titus 2:13; 1 John 5:20), and he has received the name of God, as he was glorified by the Father after his humiliation (Phil 2:9). According to the New Testament, Jesus, the Christ, is equal to God the Father, shares with the Father and the Spirit in being God, and is the unique revelation of God.

SCRIPTURE SPEAKS: CHRIST CALLED GOD

- ☐ John 1:1: "In the beginning was the Word, and the Word was with God, and the Word was God."

- ☐ John 1:18: "No one has ever seen God, but the one and only Son, who is himself God and is in closest relationship with the Father, has made him known."

- ☐ Romans 9:5: "Theirs are the patriarchs, and from them is traced the human ancestry of the Messiah, who is God over all, forever praised! Amen."

- ☐ Titus 2:12–13: "It [the grace of God] teaches us to say 'No' to ungodliness and worldly passions, and to live self-controlled, upright and godly lives in this present age, while we wait for the blessed hope—the appearing of the glory of our great God and Savior, Jesus Christ."

- ☐ 1 John 5:20: "We know also that the Son of God has come and has given us understanding, so that we may know him who is true. And we are in him who is true by being in his Son Jesus Christ. He is the true God and eternal life."

The Formulation of the Doctrine of the Trinity

"God is one essence in three persons."

These precise words are not found in the Bible. They are a formulation that could only have been articulated in the Greek philosophical tradition. Just think of it: if the gospel initially had gone southwest into Africa rather than northwest into Greece, this formulation never would have been made. African languages in general simply cannot distinguish between "essence" and "person," to say nothing of a person's "nature." While we can and should see God's providence at work in the gospel taking root in the Greco-Roman world, we should not be overly committed to the exact formulation of the doctrine of the Trinity. Rather, we must dig for its meaning—what is it supposed to convey? It is a way of expressing the reality that somehow, in Christ, we meet God. This is its positive meaning. But let us try to be more specific. Though Christ is not God the Father, he is God as much as the Father is God. They, together with the Spirit, share in being God. Yet there are not three Gods, but only one. The three—the Father, Christ, and the Spirit—are together this one God.

Why such a complicated formulation? Because in it we try to express what we find in the Bible. There are three that are said to be God, but there is only one God. The three are not the same, they are different (three different "persons"), but they all share in being God (one "essence"). So we cannot speak of God in the plural ("Gods"), but we know there is a plurality within God (Father, Son, Spirit). If this is difficult to understand, try to stretch your mind a little. When that starts to hurt, bow before the mystery of God. After all, we are trying to speak of the one true God in the universe!

SUGGESTED READING

☐ Hebrews 1:1–4. Read this section carefully and meditatively, making a list of everything you learn about Jesus.

Reflection

Hebrews 1:1–4 is a gold nugget of teaching about Jesus. Can you think of other comparable passages in the New Testament? How do passages such as John 1:1-18; Romans 1:1-6; and Colossians 1:15-20 confirm and add to what's found at the beginning of Hebrews?

_____

_____

_____

_____

Read Hebrews 1:1-4 and comparable passages. In what ways is your view of Christ too small? How do these passages enlarge your view of Christ?

_____

_____

_____

_____

Do you find the doctrine of the Trinity mysterious? If so, you are in good company! What support for this doctrine do you see developed in texts like Hebrews 1:1–3?

_____

_____

_____

_____

3

THE HUMANITY
OF CHRIST

The emphasis of this letter on just how great Christ is can
feel rather overwhelming. Nowhere else in the Bible is
Christ presented as so great and glorious. No person and
nothing else can be compared to him. In the words of a
well-known hymn, "Lord, how great thou art!" But doesn't
this create a problem? Doesn't this overwhelming greatness distance Christ from our own small world and our
daily struggles? Can we ever approach him? Is he really
interested in the tiny issues we struggle with? Can he in
any way understand our ups and downs?

Does the author realize this? Note the shifts in emphasis from the greatness of Christ to his lowliness, his meekness, his absolute equality with us? (2:9–10, 14–18; 4:15–16;
5:7–10.) Hebrews is indeed in many ways a remarkable
letter, the letter with the most glorious, divine picture
of Christ, and yet, juxtaposed with this we find the most
radical picture of his lowliness and humility. Why? In this
way the author prevents us from thinking that Christ's
greatness distances him from our world. As the glorious one he is close to us, one with us. He knows and

understands our problems because he shared our lives. He knows what it means to be a human being.

Christ Is Equal to Us

Let's take a closer look at Hebrews' picture of Christ's lowliness.

- For a short while he was made less than the angels, even though he is much greater than they are (Heb 2:9; see also 1:4–14). This means that his becoming human was in itself a humiliation.

- Jesus shared equally in human nature as we do— even to the point that he could die (Heb 2:14).

- He was made like us—again emphasizing the humiliation of becoming human. And it is emphasized: *in every way, completely* like us. Nothing human was unknown to him. Why has he been made like this? Only in this way could he "become a compassionate and trustworthy high priest" (Heb 2:17 NJB) so as to represent us before the Father. He had to experience fully what it means to be human in order to represent us before God.

- He himself was tempted and suffered like us (Heb 2:18). Why? Only in this way could he help us in our temptations. But all this means that the glorious Christ became fully human—he was tempted and suffered, just like us!

- Christ was not merely tested, but "put to the test *in exactly the same way as ourselves*" (Heb 4:15 NJB). Why? To be capable of "feeling our weaknesses" (Heb 4:15 NJB) and, in this way, to be able to represent us before the Father.

It is hard to imagine any clearer and more radical way to say that Christ knows us and understands our weaknesses and sufferings because he fully shared in our humanity. And there is more!

- In Hebrews 5:7–9, the author is clearly referring to Gethsemane. Here, in stronger language, he emphasizes Christ's suffering. Christ cried out in tears to be saved from his coming death. And then the climax: through these sufferings, he learned obedience, and in this way he became perfect!

  Maybe we can understand this in the following way. As the eternal Son of God Christ did not know what it means to obey. God never has to obey. No one ever commanded him to do anything. So how would he know what it means to obey? In becoming human Christ experienced this. He had to obey God and go to the cross even though he feared going (Matt 26:38–39). His obedience was not easy. In the end, the glorious Christ knows fully what it is to be human. Therefore you may know he is capable of feeling your weaknesses (4:15).

Far from Christ's humanity detracting from his magnificence, it enhances it! He is bigger than we thought, fully divine and fully human. This should give us great confidence in approaching him in prayer and with any concerns we may have. Go to him. Trust him. He *understands* because he is fully human, and he *can* help because he is gloriously divine.

Christ Is without Sin

The author of this letter is clear on the fact that Christ is fully human. He was made less than the angels, tempted exactly as we are, suffered under this temptation, learned what obedience is—fully human, but with one exception: he did not sin (4:15; 7:26–27). This raises a tough, theological question: Could he sin? Was he capable of sinning?

Among Christians there are two opposing answers:

- Surely not. Christ could not sin, because he was the Son of God, himself divine.

- Surely. He could indeed sin, because he was fully human.

"Surely not"—he is glorious, divine; he bears the very stamp of God's nature. Surely God cannot sin. With this response people feel they honor him in his greatness. "Yes, surely he could"—he was tempted in exactly the same way as we are, and he even suffered under temptation (2:18; 4:15). With this response people also feel they honor him. If he could not sin, was he really tempted? If sinning is impossible, what power would temptation have? If he could not sin, does he really know how we suffer under temptation? And what would 2:18 then mean: "For the suffering he himself passed through while being put to the test enables him to help others when they are being put to the test" (NJB)? Again, if he could not sin, why did Satan take the trouble of tempting him to sin (Matt 4:1–11)?

In my view the right answer to this difficult question is that he could have sinned but did not. Surely it is even more to Christ's glory if he could sin but resisted every temptation. It means that we can trust his ability to help us in our temptation. He knows how to resist! If he could not sin, it is hard to see why the Bible would even mention that he did not.

Both Divine and Human—an Unbearable Tension?

This letter confirms both the divinity and the humanity of Christ. Christ had two natures, one divine and one human. But wouldn't this have created an almost-unbearable tension, much like having to live two lives, a divine life and a human life? God and humans are radically different. So how could Christ live one fully integrated life? This challenge of interpretation confronts us with two questions:

- Why do we have this strange formulation about Christ having two natures?

- How was it possible for him to live such a complicated life made up of opposite natures? Can God and a human being live in one person?

The answer to question one is found in many places in the New Testament but most of all in Hebrews, where both his divinity and his humanity are clearly pictured. To formulate this, Hebrews uses the concept of "nature," meaning something like "character" or "disposition." But all this simply means that Christ is both divine and human.

The second question is both interesting and challenging. How was it possible for Christ to keep two such vastly different natures together? Aren't God and humans totally different? Did Jesus in fact live two different lives? Did he do some things as God (miracles, exorcisms) and some as a man (weeping, being thirst, dying)?

Some do interpret Christ's life in this double way: he did some things as God and others as a human being. As God he did miracles, but as a human being he suffered and died. As God he knew everything, but as a human being he did not know the time of his return.

But is it possible that we are looking at this from entirely the wrong angle? Is it true that God and humans

SCRIPTURE SPEAKS: CHRIST AS THE IMAGE OF GOD

- ☐ 2 Corinthians 4:4: "The god of this age has blinded the minds of unbelievers, so that they cannot see the light of the gospel that displays the glory of Christ, who is the image of God. 5 For what we preach is not ourselves, but Jesus Christ as Lord, and ourselves as your servants for Jesus' sake."

- ☐ Colossians 1:15: "The Son is the image of the invisible God, the firstborn over all creation."

- ☐ Hebrews 1:3: "He [the Son] is the reflection of God's glory and bears the impress of God's own being, sustaining all things by his powerful command; and now that he has purged sins away, he has taken his seat at the right hand of the divine Majesty on high."

are necessarily, totally different? Aren't they rather close? Humans were created in the image of God (Gen 1:26–27). "Image" presupposes resemblance. We can call it analogy, some sort of resemblance, a restricted resemblance, but surely it is still a resemblance. This resemblance is presupposed right through the New Testament in the "as" phrases: forgive *as* God has forgiven; be merciful *as* our Father is merciful; be holy *as* God is holy (Eph 4:32; Luke 6:36; 1 Pet 1:15).

Back to Jesus. There is no indication in the New Testament that Jesus lived two lives or that he experienced an inner tension. If humans are supposed to be God's image, showing forth God's way of life and his values, then Jesus was able to reveal both God *and* humanity in one fully integrated life. In loving, caring, and sharing, he showed forth both who God is and how humans should be. That is also why he is often called the image of God (2 Cor 4:4; Col 1:15; Heb 1:3). This implies that our resemblance to God should be one of disposition, attitude, values, way of life.

Being God's image means that Jesus revealed who God is and who humans are—or, to put it more clearly, how humans should be. Jesus is a window, through which we can see what human life looks like when lived as God intended. We always need to add "should be" because we are not what God meant us to be. God meant us to be his image, to reflect his way of life, but neither Israel nor we have done what God intended. Therefore God has again created a human, again after his image, and is showing us in his life an example of what/how he intended us to be.

However, Jesus is not only an example to us. Through the Holy Spirit he unites us to himself so that we share in his life (John 15:3; Gal 2:19–20; Col 3:4). In this way God, in the end, makes it possible for us to be his image, not by what *we* do but by sharing in *his* life. I reflect God's image through the life I participate in: Christ, his image.

SUGGESTED READING

Read through these verses to see how God wants us to reflect his image:

- ☐ Colossians 3:13
- ☐ Ephesians 4:32
- ☐ 1 Peter 1:15–16
- ☐ 1 John 1:5–7
- ☐ Luke 6:36
- ☐ Matthew 5:48

Read through these verses on reflecting Christ:

- ☐ John 13:34
- ☐ John 20:21
- ☐ Ephesians 5:2, 25
- ☐ 1 John 3:3, 7

Reflection

What, in your view, does the Bible mean by describing us as made "in God's image"?

_____

_____

_____

How does the magnificent Christ help us in this respect?

_____

_____

_____

How does Christ being fully human affect the way you relate to God?

_____

_____

_____

Was it possible for Christ to sin? What is your answer to this mysterious question?

_____

_____

_____

_____

Take time to think and pray. How can the Spirit build your life into this image of God and Christ?

_____

_____

_____

4

THE MAGNIFICENCE OF CHRIST

By far the biggest part of the letter is devoted to the greatness of Christ, how Christ is greater than anyone and anything in the Old Testament. An impressive list of these "greater than" statements is found in Hebrews.

The Angels (1:4–14)

In the long list of Old Testament entities presented in this letter, the angels are mentioned first. This also has symbolic meaning, for they are heavenly beings and thus greater than human beings. They have direct access to God. Only God is higher than them. So, in putting Christ above them, the author confirms his emphasis on the divinity of Christ we saw in 1:1–4. In supporting the greatness of Christ above the angels, the writer uses the Old Testament extensively. In Psalm 2, the Messiah is called "the Son," a title never used for the angels. And in Psalm 45, he is called both "God" and "king" (45:7–8, 11–15) — again, titles never used for the angels.

In Hebrews 1:14, a small gem lies hidden. The angels are ministering spirits serving believers. The angels are far above humans; nevertheless, they are to serve the needs of inferior beings, us humans. This implies that highness in the heavenly realm does not exclude humble service. This is seen most vividly in Christ not coming to be served but to serve humankind (Mark 10:48). Thus, one way in which Christ is greater than the angels is that he is a greater *servant!* And Christ wants us to follow his example (Phil 2:3–8). So this becomes part of the constitution of the kingdom of God.

JESUS IS GREATER THAN ...

☐   Christ is greater than the *angels,* though the angels, as heavenly beings, are greater than anyone on earth.

☐   Christ is greater than *Moses and Joshua,* the founders of the people of Israel. To the Jews, Moses was *the* man of God.

☐   Christ is greater than the temple, the priests, the sacrifices, the feasts—the Old Testament's entire liturgy, or way of worshiping the Lord.

☐   Christ brings a better law, but the law was the God-given way of life for his people.

☐   Christ introduces a superior covenant, even though the covenant at Sinai was given by God's own hand to Moses as his "everlasting" will (Deut 5:6–21).

This list represents the entire way of life and virtually everything Israel believed and had to obey in the name of God. But Christ is more—much, much more!

Moses (3:1-6)

Christ is greater than Moses. The angels did not play such an important role in the Old Testament. But Christ greater than Moses? Moses is *the* person in the Old Testament.

The most important part of the Jewish Bible is the first five books of *Moses,* and the law, which is God's will for his people, is the law of *Moses.* In these books we find more lofty things written about Moses than about any other human being. God himself said: "When there is a prophet among you, I, the LORD, reveal myself to them in visions, I speak to them in dreams. But this is not true of my servant Moses; he is faithful in all my house. With him I speak face to face, clearly and not in riddles; he sees the form of the LORD" (Num 12:6-8). The last sentence is referring to Exodus 33:23, and in that same chapter we read that God spoke to Moses like a friend (33:11).

All of this strongly supports the Jewish view that Moses was to be honored more highly than any other person. The Jews would name Moses and God in one breath and put Moses on the same level as the temple which is the house of God (Acts 6:11, 13). This means that proclaiming Christ as much greater than Moses is to rank him higher than any human being. This writer compares Christ to Moses by the position they have in "God's house," which in this case is the family of believers (3:2, 5, 6):

- Moses was faithful as a *servant in* God's house ...

- ... but Christ is faithful as *the Son over* God's house.

What a difference between a servant and "the Son," between serving in and ruling over God's house.

It is important to see that directly following this comparison, we find the encouragement for the readers to hold firmly on to what they believe (3:6) and the grave warning not to turn "away from the living God" (3:12). Why? Because "we have come to share in Christ, if indeed we hold our original conviction firmly to the end" (3:14). This implies that the comparisons between Christ and the Old Testament figures are not merely theoretical exercises but a call for personal decisions from the readers to keep to the faith they have accepted, which again implies that there must have been the grave danger of believers letting go of Christ.

Joshua and Sabbath Rest (4:1-11)

This comparison is not between Christ and Joshua in person, but rather between Christ and what Joshua meant to Israel. Joshua had to guide Israel to settle in Canaan, but because of their disobedience they failed to enter the rest God has promised. Now the author compares that rest to the rest now offered through Christ (4:1, 6) and stresses that the believers should enter this rest and not fail through disobedience (4:11). "Entering" means keeping to the faith, persevering (3:14). In chapter 6 we will return to this issue and explore the question of what happens if we do not persevere. It is important to note that it is not only our individual responsibility to enter but also to see that our fellow believers do so (3:13). We are the house or family of God and as such bear responsibility toward one another.

Sabbath Keeping

The emphasis on sabbath and rest raises the question: how should Christians keep the Sabbath commandment today?

"A Sabbath-rest" (4:9). Here we read that "there remains, then, a Sabbath-rest for the people of God." What does that mean in terms of Sabbath-keeping? We here have the one and only use of the word "Sabbath-rest" in the New Testament. This is the rest God offers after Israel failed to enter the rest in Canaan. It is likely that this refers back to the fourth of the Ten Commandments regarding Sabbath keeping. If so, it is the only reference to this commandment in the New Testament after the resurrection of Christ. This in itself is striking, as there are many references to most of the other Ten Commandments (for instance, Eph 4:25–5:5; Col 3:5–9). The non-appearance of the fourth commandment coincides with the fact that after the resurrection of Christ, no mention is made of Christians keeping the Sabbath.

There are, of course, a number of references to Paul attending Sabbath meetings in synagogues during his missionary journeys (Acts 13:14; 14:1; 17:1, 10; 18:4; 19:8). Why did he go there, and what did he do? "Paul went into the synagogue, and on three Sabbath days he reasoned with them [the Jews] from the Scriptures, explaining and proving that the Messiah had to suffer and rise from the dead. 'This Jesus I am proclaiming to you is the Messiah,' he said" (Acts 17:2–3). This was no gathering of Christians, but Jews. Paul visited them on the Sabbath, in the synagogue, as it was the only day he could get hold of them as a group and try to convince them about Jesus.

It seems clear that the Gentile Christians did not keep the Sabbath. If they had, it would have become a problem the apostles would have had to address in their letters. Slave owners would surely not have allowed their slaves, all of a sudden, to keep one day of rest every week. But there is no indication that such a problem arose.

It seems that Christians started special worship events on the first day of the week, our Sunday. But they did this after hours, either at night or early in the morning. Paul spoke to the believers in Troas at night (Acts 20:7–8). We read of specific things they did on the first day of the week (John 20:19, 26; 1 Cor 16:2), which later is called "the Lord's Day" (Rev 1:10). But these events are never related to the Sabbath or the fourth commandment. It seems obvious that early Christians did not simply change the day from Saturday to our Sunday but because of Jesus's resurrection on the first day of the week started a special observation of Sunday. This day differed from the Sabbath-rest commandment.

But what happened to the fourth commandment? All the others remained intact. There is more to it than this. They did not merely remain intact; they were all radicalized. Jesus started this, and Paul continued along the same lines. Jesus emphatically announced that no command, not even the smallest letter in the law, will disappear "until everything is accomplished," the reason being that he did not come to abolish the law but to fulfill it (Matt 5:17–18). The sixth commandment reads, "Do not commit murder," but Jesus extends its limits to anger and swear words (Matt 5:21–22). This means I can murder someone by the words I use or by the way I look at him or her. Jesus also refers to the seventh commandment, "Do not commit adultery," and warns us that we can commit adultery by the way we look at a person—thus in a spiritual way, in our hearts (Matt 5:27-30). Paul continues along the same lines. About those who steal, he writes they should stop doing this and start "doing something useful with their own hands, that they may have something to share with those in need" (Eph 4:28). This seems to me to imply that whenever I withhold whatever I could give to someone in need, I am stealing from him or her. This is the "new" meaning of the Ten Commandments in the New Testament. One may call it a spiritualization or radicalization of the Ten Commandments.

But what then of the fourth commandment? Did it simply disappear? Not if we believe Jesus. Not even a small letter in the law would disappear. Could the "Sabbath-rest" of Hebrews 4:9 help us? In fact I find no other clear reference in the New Testament after the resurrection of Jesus I could call on. This Sabbath rest is related to the eternal rest of God himself. We will ourselves rest when we enter God's rest (4:10). God's rest is permanent. He created everything and then rested on the seventh day (Gen 1). He never created again. He permanently rests from creating. So believers should rest from their own work (Heb 4:10). What work? The work of disobedience. This is the implication of the following verse: that Israel did not enter God's rest because of their disobedience. To me this comes down to two things:

- The fourth commandment has been radicalized like all the others in that the one day of rest per week has been turned into a permanent rest.

- The rest from work has also been radicalized by turning it into rest from disobedience, from sin.

So keeping the Sabbath for us means to rest permanently from our sin, to serve God wholeheartedly all through the week and all through our lives.

And Sunday?

Why Sunday as a special day? Wouldn't Friday have been a better option, the day Jesus died to save us? Isn't that the heart of the gospel? But what would have happened if Jesus died but remained dead and not raised? His story would have gone to the grave with the apostles. Nothing would have remained of his teachings and example. Why does Paul relate Christ's *resurrection* to our justification and deliverance from sin? Didn't Christ *die* for our sins and rose only to conquer death? Surely, but ...

- "He was delivered over to death for our sins and was *raised* to life for our *justification*" (Rom 4:25, emphasis mine).

- "And if Christ has not been *raised* ... you are still in your *sins*" (1 Cor 15:17, emphasis mine).

Clearly this implies that his resurrection bears directly on the meaningfulness of his cross.

- God raised him to show that he has accepted his death as atonement for our sins.

- This means that the atoning value of the cross depends on his resurrection.

- That means that the salvific value of Friday depends on Sunday.

- That again means that the day to celebrate our salvation is indeed Sunday.

Here again it is worth pausing to contemplate the enormity of Christ and what he has done—and is doing—for us! It is a good thing to make going to church on Sundays a habit, but we do need to be reminded of just how significant is this gathering as his people on Sunday. We gather as those for whom he has worked—and desires—to be entirely free of sin and full of goodness. And his work is not just directed at us but at the entire creation. Truly he is the magnificent Christ.

The Temple

The temple is but one in a series of interrelated Old Testament concepts like the priests, the sacrifices, the law, and the covenant. These bring us to the heart of the message of Hebrews. Together, they form the actual point of comparison between Christ and the Old Testament. Why these? Because they formed the heart of Israel's worship. This is the reason why we will first examine them together before unpacking them one by one.

In the first four chapters the author dealt one by one with the different persons he compared with Christ: angels, Moses, Joshua. But now he will be dealing with these five concepts intertwined in chapters 5 and 7–10, the major part of the letter. This way of simultaneously

dealing with these concepts is not strange, as together
they constitute the worship of Israel. Reading through
chapters 5 and 7–10, several things stand out:

- Christ is more, better, greater, more effective
  than anything and everything in the worship
  of Israel.

- But Christ does not only improve on these, he
  simply replaces them. He does not add yet
  another sacrifice. He replaces all sacrifices by
  his own.

- He does not build yet another temple. He offers
  himself in the only real one in heaven.

- This means that these elements are relativized.
  How on earth could the blood of bulls and goats
  take away sins (10:4)?

- As a result of this, even Moses is relativized.

- But what then happens to the meaningfulness
  and usefulness of the Old Testament itself
  (Heb 5)?

In the later times of the Old Testament there were a few
temples over and above the one in Jerusalem—the three
built in the Northern Kingdom, in Gilgal, Bethel, and
Dan. But these were heavily criticized by the prophets as
illegitimate (Amos 4:4–5; 1 Kgs 12:26–33). The temple in
Jerusalem was the only legitimate one, the true "house
of God." There, and only there, true sacrifices were made.
But Christ brings the real sacrifice on a hill in Jerusalem
called Golgotha, an unclean hill where no sacrifice has

ever been made. How could this sacrifice ever be acceptable, let alone the only true one?

The answer in the Letter to the Hebrews is remarkable. The temple in Jerusalem never was the true temple. At its best it was a copy or a shadow made by human hands of "what is in heaven" (8:5; see also 9:23, 24). In two respects it could never have been the real or true temple: it was merely a copy of the true one in heaven, and it was made by human hands. The implication clearly is that the priests of the Old Testament indeed never made sacrifices in the true temple.

Christ was the first priest to do this. But has he been sacrificed in the true temple, in heaven? Or rather on an unclean hill outside Jerusalem, Golgotha? No. According to Hebrews, he did not make his sacrifice there. "For Christ did not enter a sanctuary made with human hands … he entered heaven itself, now to appear for us in God's presence" (9:24). Also he "serves in the sanctuary, the true tabernacle set up by the Lord, not by a mere human being" (8:2). How are we to understand this? Remember the animals were indeed sacrificed on the altar in the temple, but they were killed, slaughtered outside the temple. In the same way Christ is killed outside the true temple in heaven, but in the ascension he took his sacrifice, himself, into the true temple in heaven to the Father. So Christ and he alone brought the one and only true sacrifice in the one and only true temple in heaven.

The Priests

Priests and sacrifices are so intertwined in Hebrews that they can scarcely be dealt with separately. The

comparison between Christ and the priests is very interesting. In terms of the law Christ could not have been a
priest, to say nothing of being the real, true high priest.
Priests came from the tribe of Levi, while Christ was from
the tribe of Judah (7:13, 14). But way back in history there
was a strange figure called Melchizedek, "priest of God
Most High" (Gen 14:18). And Christ was a priest "in the
order of Melchizedek" (Heb 7:11).

This order of priesthood had some important features
that favored Christ. The ordinary priests became priests
through descendance, but Christ because of the quality of
his life ("on the basis of the power of an indestructible life,"
7:16). Also there was no succession in this priestly order
as in the order of the ordinary priests. So Christ "has a
permanent priesthood" (7:24). This enabled him "to save
completely those who come to God through him, because
he always lives to intercede for them" (7:25). Yet another
advantage of Christ was that he was sinless. The ordinary
high priests were sinners like the people. They had first
to offer a sacrifice for their own sin, and only then for
the people. But Christ "sacrificed for their sins once for
all when he offered himself" (7:27). "Such a high priest
truly meets our need—one who is holy, blameless, pure,
set apart from sinners, exalted above the heavens" (7:26).

The Unity of Humankind

One aspect of the comparison between Christ and the
priests is striking. The argument of the author is that
Christ's priesthood was better than that of the Levitical
priests. Why? Because Abraham gave Melchizedek a tenth
of the plunder (7:4), and then Abraham was blessed by

Melchizedek. The author argues as follows. One gives a tenth to a superior, and in return the superior blesses the inferior. So Melchizedek was greater than Abraham. But Abraham had a great-grandson, Levi, from whom the priests were descended. Thus Levi in fact gave a tenth to Melchizedek because when Abraham gave a tenth, "Levi was still in the body of his ancestor" (7:10).

This will seem very strange to most readers, especially to those Westerners with strongly individualistic worldviews. But the author to the Hebrews was convinced that the posterity of a person is present in the person and somehow participates in what the person does. Levi participated in Abraham's giving of a tenth to Melchizedek. Christ is a priest in the order of Melchizedek, so he is more important than the Levitical priests.

Original Sin

This principal of posterity being included in an ancestor and *somehow* participating in what the ancestor is doing is also found elsewhere in the Bible. Just think of Paul's comparison of Adam and Christ (Rom 5:12–21). The point Paul is making is that somehow all humans participated in Adam's sin and so are under God's judgment. As in the case of Levi they were already "in the body of Adam," so to speak, when he and Eve sinned. This is more or less the background of the doctrine of original sin. In the history of Christian thought theologians have developed different ways of accounting for our being connected with the sin of the first couple. Some have argued that Adam is the representative head of humanity, whereas others have argued that sin is passed on from the first couple through human generation. It is obvious that one can object against this. How can it be that I am under God's judgment for sin that I have not committed? Isn't this a strange view of humanity, because of which I am judged? What becomes of human responsibility?

But perhaps we have stopped too early and have not read through to see the actual point Paul is making. Paul did not write Romans 5 because of Adam, but because of Christ. The same principle of "all in one" and "one for all" also relates to the work of Christ. As the sin of Adam is imputed to me, so also the righteousness of Christ.

- Because of what Adam did, I am under God's judgment.

- But because of what Christ did, I am acquitted.

"Just as one trespass resulted in condemnation for all people, so also one righteous act resulted in justification and life for all" (Rom 5:18). However much I hate being under God's judgment for the sin of someone else, I love being forgiven and justified because of the righteousness of Someone else. To "inherit" sin seems unjust, but I gladly bear with it because of "inheriting" grace and righteousness.

Sacrifices

Christ is much greater than the priests of the Old Testament. But exactly how much only becomes clear when we look at the sacrifices.

- The priests had to bring the sacrifices regularly, which implies that they were not effective (Heb 10:2–4).

- Instead of really cleansing people from sin, the repeated bringing of the sacrifices rather reminded people of their sin (10:2–3).

- Instead of liberating people's consciousness from sin, the sacrifices only cleansed them outwardly (9:13, 14).

- Why? "It is impossible for the blood of bulls and goats to take away sins" (10:4).

- In fact the very reason why these sacrifices were repeatedly brought was because they did not remove sin (10:11).

Over against these defects the author puts the one sacrifice of Christ.

- He needed to bring his sacrifice only once because it really takes away sin (9:14).

- He needed to bring only one sacrifice because he himself was sinless so he needed first to bring a sacrifice for his own sin (7:27; 9:12).

There is yet one other difference. We are so accustomed to this that we barely realize it. The priests received the offerings from the people and then put them on the altar as a sacrifice. It was the people who gave the sacrifices, not the priests. The priests in fact benefited from the sacrifices. Most of the meat and wheat was for their sustenance. And Christ? Who gave him the offering he had to put on the altar? How did he benefit from it? Just think about it for a minute. He did not receive an offering from the people who sinned, like the priests. He had to find one himself. What did he find? Himself!

If Christ is the one and only priest in history who sacrificed himself, then there simply is no way in which the
priests can meaningfully be compared to him. He was not
merely *greater* but *much* greater than they. He was priest
on a different level, of a different order. This is what it
really means for him to be of the order of Melchizedek,
incomparable to anyone else.

Law and Covenant

These two are not specific things, like priests and sacrifices. They represent the basic structure of Israel's relationship with God. In the New Testament the "law" mostly
refers to the Torah, the first five books of the Bible. These
were the rules of conduct for the people of Israel, and
they truly came from God. The Sadducees stuck to these
as the only word of God, and while the Pharisees were
more liberal and also accepted the other books of the Old
Testament, even to them the Torah was the actual word
of God.

As with the sacrifices, the author of Hebrews had serious questions about the law. "It was weak and useless (for
the law made nothing perfect)" (7:18–19). Christ is "a better
hope ... by which we draw near to God" (7:19). "The law
is only a shadow of the good things that are coming—not
the realities themselves" (10:1). This means that Jews had
to choose between the law as an end in itself and Christ as
the one who fulfills the law. This surely was a hard choice
for a Jew. After all, the law was given by God's own hand
to Moses. We will return to this in chapter 5.

This also pertains to the covenant. According to
Hebrews Christ became the guarantor and mediator of a

new covenant with better promises because of what was wrong with the first covenant (7:22; 8:6, 7). Now, this covenant does not refer back to Abraham, but to Sinai, as Jeremiah clearly points out (Jer 31:31–34). The Sinai covenant and the law are in direct relationship to each other. The covenant determines the relationship between God and Israel, and the law determines the way Israel should live in this relationship.

Way back in the Old Testament, we read of a new covenant to be established because Israel broke the first one (Jer 31:31–34). This new covenant is directly related to the law. In the new covenant the law will be written on the hearts of the people and not merely on stone tablets. This means that the law will not only be known by the people, but they will live according to it. Hebrews refers specifically to Jeremiah 31 and states that this change has come about by Christ (8:7–13).

Old Covenant, New Covenant, Covenant with Abraham

It is important to distinguish clearly between the old covenant and the new on the one side and the covenant with Abraham on the other. Hebrews works with the old and the new covenant. No reference is made to the covenant with Abraham. The covenant with Abraham is concluded in Genesis (Gen 12–17), while the old covenant—that is, the covenant of the law—was established at Sinai after the exodus from Egypt (Exod 19–20). Jeremiah very specifically refers to the covenant at *Sinai,* the covenant God made with Israel "when [he] took them by the hand to lead them out of Egypt" (Jer 31:32). The covenant with Abraham is of a different nature. There is never any suggestion that this one was or will be abrogated or changed; indeed, it seems still fully intact (Gal 3:17). Christ is the "child" of Abraham (Gal 3:16 NLT), and through baptism we are taken up into this covenant (Gal 3:26–29). This is the covenant of grace. Abraham is the father of all believers (Rom 4:16), and all believers are sons of Abraham (Gal 3:7). Whoever has faith "is blessed along with Abraham" (Gal 3:9).

But the question then is: what is the relationship between the new covenant in Christ and the covenant of grace concluded with Abraham? Just look at the new covenant. There are two important elements: God's law will be written on our hearts, and he will be our God and we will be his people (Jer 31:33; Heb 8:10). To have his law written on our hearts means truly to believe—like Abraham did. That God is our God and we are his people is exactly the main content of the covenant with Abraham. This means that the introduction of the new covenant is in essence the reaffirmation of the covenant with Abraham.

But why is this reaffirmation necessary? Did something happen to this covenant since its introduction in Genesis? Yes. God concluded the covenant with Abraham. It came down to the fact that Abraham believed in God, and that God is his God, and he and his posterity are God's people. Four centuries later (Gal 3:17), God led Israel out of Egypt and gave the law at Sinai. This is called the covenant of the law. This simply meant that God now gave his covenant people a rule of conduct. They, as God's people, should live according to the law. But along the way Israel began to misunderstand this rule of conduct, this covenant of the law. Instead of living in a faith relationship with God and therefore living according to the law, they started trusting in the law to save them. They tried in every way to fulfill the law so as to become acceptable to God.

In exactly this way the covenant of grace and faith, the covenant with Abraham, disappeared from their lives, and the law became a curse to the people. This is why it is called the old covenant that is to be replaced by a new one. The new one, then, is the reaffirmation of the covenant of grace, the covenant with Abraham. This means that we get two perspectives in the New Testament:

- Hebrews, looking from the side of the law, calls it a new covenant.

- Paul, looking from the side of faith, calls it the covenant with Abraham.

It is obvious that these insights into the covenant with Abraham will influence our views on baptism and maybe especially the question of infant baptism.

The Addressees

Hebrews is an overwhelming expression of the superiority of Christ. Looking at the list of comparisons it seems that virtually everything of importance in the Old Testament has been included.

- The list starts with the angels that are closest to God,

- then the two founders of the people of Israel,

- then its entire worship system,

- and ends with the basic structure of its relationship with God—covenant and law.

Why this overwhelming emphasis on the greatness of Christ? And why is it set over against the Old Testament, against virtually every important person, office, or structure in the Old Testament? To whom is the author writing this letter? And why? Does he fear the addressees may let go of Christ and return to the Old Testament form of the faith?

In the days of the early church there were only two groups of Christians who possibly could consider this return: the Jewish Christians and the "God fearers" like Cornelius (Acts 10:1). The latter were gentiles who had accepted the Old Testament faith in full or in part and later on became Christians. These two groups could at some stage and for various reasons reconsider their decision and go back to the synagogue, to the Jewish religion. One possible reason is that in some situations Christians were persecuted, while the Jewish religion was tolerated by the Roman government. Some of these Christians who were persecuted could therefore consider returning to their former faith to escape persecution.

This seems exactly the reason why this letter was written. Even the heading itself suggests this: the Letter to the *Hebrews*. Though this word does not occur in the letter itself, it has from very early on been called "the Letter to the Hebrews" exactly because it was accepted that it was written to Hebrews, meaning Jewish Christians. In all probability the addressees also included some "God fearers," as these were the main group of converts on Paul's missionary journeys.

Relevance for Today?

Is this letter still relevant to our situation today? Are there meaningful numbers of Christians who consider leaving Christ for Old Testament religion? No, though there are a number of Christians, often very dedicated ones, who do go back to many of the features of the Old Testament religion like the feasts, the Sabbath, the trumpet, the Hebrew names of God. Still, for many good reasons this book remains of exceptional importance.

Christians are the most persecuted religious group in the world today, a fact that many in the West find hard to take seriously. In such contexts it will be tempting to abandon the faith and submit to cultural pressures, a context to which Hebrews speaks with exceptional power. In the West it is tempting for many to drift slowly away from Christ into the easy, everything-goes consumerism of our day. Again, Hebrews speaks to this situation.

To all of us Hebrews continues to speak in so many ways. First, it speaks because of the wonderful picture we here have of the glorious Lord and Savior we serve. How great he is! Second, it helps us formulate our positions against those theologians who want to "demote" Christ and see in him only a "good person." Doing this breaks our link with the apostles and the early Christians. What we need today is not a *demotion* of Christ but rather an *elevation* up to the level of Hebrews. Third, the emphasis on Christ's meekness and humanity assures us that he knows our tears and sorrows, our weaknesses and troubles, that in fact he has himself experienced all these and so he both can and will care for us. Fourth, it enables us to develop a refined view of the meaning of the Old

THE MAGNIFICENCE OF CHRIST   51

Testament. Hebrews refers back to the Old Testament more than any other book in the New Testament, and it does so in a very clear way. We learn that Christ is more—much, much more—than anyone and anything in the Old Testament but also that the Old Testament still has meaning for us today. Finally, it will be a tremendous guide for those who return to Old Testament practices like the feasts, the Sabbath, the trumpet, the obligation to use only the Hebrew names of God and Jesus.

SUGGESTED READING

☐   Hebrews 5

☐   Hebrews 7–10

Reflection

"Better than" sums up the message of Hebrews. See if you can recall all the things Jesus is said to be better than in Hebrews.

_____

_____

_____

_____

_____

What things are we tempted today to think are better than Jesus? How is he in fact better than them?

_____

_____

_____

_____

Do you agree with our interpretation of Sabbath and Sunday (Heb 4:8-11)? Does it make the fourth commandment more meaningful to you?

_____

_____

_____

_____

Which is the old covenant that has been abrogated: Abraham or Sinai? Explain.

_____

_____

_____

_____

5

THE USE OF THE OLD TESTAMENT IN HEBREWS

The basic message of Hebrews is that Christ is incomparably greater than anyone and anything in the Old Testament and that the Jewish or Gentile believers should not even think of returning to Old Testament religion. In principle this is in line with the convictions of most Christians. But it creates a problem when the author of this letter goes further than this. The message is not only that Christ is much greater than anyone and anything in the Old Testament and not only that Christ replaced some of the Old Testament features of worship. Rather, the message is that some very important features in the Old Testament are no longer effective—and even that some never were.

Let us have a look at the author's negative views.

- The priests had to bring the sacrifices regularly, which implies that they were not effective (10:2–4).

- Instead of really cleansing people from sin, the repeated bringing of the sacrifices reminded people of their sin (10:2-3).

- Instead of liberating people's consciousness from sin, the sacrifices only cleansed them outwardly (9:13-14).

- "It is impossible for the blood of bulls and goats to take away sins" (10:4).

- The very reason why these sacrifices were brought repeatedly was because they did not really remove sin (10:11).

- The law "was weak and useless (for the law made nothing perfect)" (7:18-19).

- "The law is only a shadow of the good things that are coming—not the realities themselves" (10:1).

Isn't this rather rough? Is it an overreaction simply to make the point as strongly as possible that Christ is much greater than anyone and anything in the Old Testament? But doesn't this way of making the point totally negate our view of the Old Testament? Most of us are convinced that the Old Testament is part and parcel of the Bible and is deeply meaningful to us as such. It is not easy to find satisfying answers to these questions. Let us first work through the range of uses of the Old Testament in this letter.

The Positive Use of the Old Testament in Hebrews

It is clear that this letter uses the Old Testament much more than any other book in the New Testament. Check this for yourself by counting the number of references to the Old Testament at the bottom of the pages in Hebrews in the TNIV or any other translation that lists them. While the author wants to convince the readers to hold on to Christ, he is concerned throughout to show how the Old Testament is superseded by Christ.

This raises an interesting question: why did the author not use the Old Testament in the same way as Paul? Paul aimed to convince the Jews that Christ is the *fulfillment* of the Old Testament by being the promised Messiah. To Paul it would be completely logical for the Jews to accept Christ simply because they are Jews—Christ is the fulfillment of their own Scriptures. Thus Paul creates a direct link with the Old Testament. Why does the author of Hebrews not use the same approach? We cannot be sure, but the author chooses the negative way and in this way strongly relativizes the Old Testament.

But there is more to it than this. It is not true that this author is *only* negative toward the Old Testament. Let us now look at his *positive* use of the Old Testament:

- He starts with a comparison between the prophets of the Old Testament and Jesus (1:1-2). There is nothing negative about the prophets. On the contrary, he states that God spoke through them, though even here Christ is much greater than they.

- His reference to the angels has no negative tone, although even here Christ is much greater (Heb 1:5–14).

- Again, his reference to Moses is not negative (Heb 3).

- His use of Melchizedek from Genesis 14 is completely positive (Heb 7).

All of this implies that we started incorrectly. Our point was that he uses the Old Testament negatively. That now seems *not* to be correct. The New Testament regularly sees Old Testament characters and institutions as types or figures that are fulfilled in the New Testament, an emphasis we also find in Hebrews. What is true is that the author is negative toward certain features of the Sinai covenant— not the Old Testament as such. His criticism is against the temple-priests-sacrifices-covenant-law complex of features. But there is even more to his positive use of the Old Testament.

The Position of Hebrews 11

This famous chapter is overwhelmingly positive in relation to the Old Testament. It is worth careful examination. Let us start with three things:

- The position of this chapter in the letter.

- The beginning of this chapter.

- The words immediately following the chapter.

Its Position

This chapter is immediately after the important middle section of this letter, chapters 7–10. As it is so positive about the Old Testament, it forms a sharp contrast with that middle section. Was this carefully planned by the author? Was it the author's intention to show that negativity is not a principle but pertains to specific features? Is this the reason for the remarkably positive attitude toward the Old Testament in this chapter?

Its Beginning

The chapter starts with a "definition" of faith: "Now faith is confidence in what we hope for and assurance about what we do not see" (11:1).

The point he makes is that we still do not see and experience the things we hope for. As Paul writes, "We live by faith, not by sight" (2 Cor 5:7). Why does the author write this here? Is it because the readers of this letter are deeply distressed about the suffering they have faced since they have accepted Christ, that they experience nothing of the glory of the coming Messiah? Does he want to tell them that we still look forward to the coming glory, that it is still part of our faith and hope, and that therefore suffering should not upset them? Does he want to say that suffering is part and parcel of being a Christian? Paul is clear and emphatic about this (Acts 14:22; 2 Tim 3:12). In defining faith as "confidence in what we hope for," is he opposing a sort of "prosperity gospel"?

If all this is true, it means that the place and the structure of chapter 11 is carefully planned.

The End of Chapter 11 and the Beginning of Chapter 12

And now the transition from chapter 11 to chapter 12. It is possible that here we have the high point or climax of the entire letter. Look at the close of chapter 11: the believers of the Old Testament are "commended for their faith, yet none of them received what had been promised." They had suffered terribly for their faith but persevered (11:32–40). This is a strong message to readers.

But why have they not received what they have hoped for? Because God "planned something better for us so that only together with us would they be made perfect" (11:40). This means that the author now relates positively to the Old Testament, just as do Paul and Peter. The Old Testament is open ended because the believers have been waiting for something to happen. What new still had to happen? What was missing in the Old Testament? Why couldn't they reach perfection without the New Testament? Because Christ had not yet come. He completes everything.

The Beginning of Chapter 12

We, like the Old Testament believers, have a race to run. Instead of now hesitating, growing weary, and losing heart (12:3), readers of Hebrews should "run with perseverance ... fixing our eyes on Jesus, the pioneer and perfecter of our faith" (12:1–2). The author's point is: do as Jesus did. "For the joy set before him he endured the cross, scorning its shame, and sat down at the right hand of the throne of God" (12:2). "Consider him" (12:3)! What a call on believers who start growing weary and faint! The entire Old Testament was waiting on Jesus. Now he has come, and you have met him. Keep going. He makes the difference. Do not let go. This is yet another outstanding example of positive linking back to the Old Testament.

Hebrews 11—Its Contents

There is, in the entire New Testament, no chapter as positive about the Old Testament as Hebrews 11. Right from the start it lauds the believers of the Old Testament (11:2). He starts lauding them one by one, but in the end the list is simply too long, so he generalizes (11:32) and even refer to incidents of suffering not known to us. What does that leave us? In the main section of this letter, a sharp, negative view of some very important features in the Old Testament but, immediately following this, a hymn of praise.

Let us consider what he writes about Abraham and Moses and exactly how this fits the situation of the Hebrews.

Abraham

The author follows the story line of the Old Testament. But then he turns to a generalization: not merely Abraham, but "all these people. ... They did not receive the things promised," but they kept the faith, realizing that they are but "foreigners and strangers on earth" looking forward to what lies in the future (Heb 11:13). What a call on the Hebrews, who also are not experiencing what they expected! And then the grave warning: "If they had been thinking of the country they had left, they would have had opportunity to return" (11:15). This is a reference to

Israel during the exodus. What would have happened if they had continued longing for Egypt? A return—and the loss of everything that God had promised them. Readers of Hebrews, keep to the faith. Everything is at stake.

Moses

Moses was the most important person in the history of Israel. The Hebrews are considering going back to the Old Testament faith. Well, what did Moses do? He refused the honor of being known as the son of Pharaoh's daughter. Instead he chose to be mistreated along with the people of God. "He regarded disgrace for the sake of Christ as of greater value than the treasures of Egypt, because he was looking ahead to his reward ... He persevered because he saw him who is invisible" (11:26–27). This fits the situation of the Hebrews like a glove fits a hand. They too are suffering. They too have to look ahead to him who is invisible and to their reward.

Again, the Negativity of Hebrews toward the Old Testament

The heading is misleading, and intentionally so. We now have to realize that it is *not true* that Hebrews is negative toward the Old Testament. It is only negative about certain features in the Old Testament, which we listed at the beginning of this chapter. How are we to interpret these negative views? What is the problem?

The problem is that they are straightforwardly negative statements in principle. We do not read something like, "*afterwards it became clear* that the blood of bulls could not cleanse from sin," but the straightforward statement,

RECAP: THE AUTHOR'S NEGATIVE VIEWS

☐   The priests had to bring the sacrifices regularly, which implies that they were not effective (10:2–4).

☐   Instead of really cleansing people from sin, the repeated bringing of the sacrifices reminded people of their sin (10:2–3).

☐   Instead of liberating people's consciousness from sin, the sacrifices only cleansed them outwardly (9:13–14).

☐   "It is impossible for the blood of bulls and goats to take away sins" (10:4).

☐   The very reason why these sacrifices were brought repeatedly was because they did not really remove sin (10:11).

☐   The law "was weak and useless (for the law made nothing perfect)" (7:18–19).

☐   "The law is only a shadow of the good things that are coming—not the realities themselves" (10:1).

"It is impossible for the blood of bulls and goats to take away sins" (Heb 10:4). Not even "It *was* ..." But there was no hint in this direction in the Old Testament, not even that the value of these features was only temporal. There are at least two different ways to try to understand this: first, that Christ in any case had to come in the future, which means that everything in the Old Testament was provisional in principle. Second, Christ had such an overwhelming significance that at his coming the entire past had to be seen in his light.

The first is that everything has, in any case, been provisional and temporal. Right from the start, the sacrifices had no internal value. They were effective simply because Christ would eventually come and make them effective by his sacrifice—so the cross has retrospective value. Even the faithful were saved because of what Christ would later do. This means that without Christ the Old Testament had and still has no meaning. If these young Christians let go of Christ, even the Old Testament will lose its meaning.

But we may have some hesitation about this view. Does it not rob the Old Testament of any value in itself? Isn't it reading the Old Testament *only* in the light of the New? Why is nothing of this provisional character visible in the Old Testament—no indications that the sacrifices only had dependent value, a value only afterward to be provided? The Old Testament, read on its own, seem to have its own intrinsic value. Whatever the priests did was exactly what God ordered.

The second view is that only *afterward*, when Christ came, was it apparent that his overwhelming meaning made everything appear in a new light. Only at this stage did it become clear that certain features had no intrinsic value. For example, there is no indication in the Old Testament that Christ was involved in creating the world. It only afterward came to light. Nowhere in the Old Testament is there any hint that four important figures—the prophet, the servant, the messiah, and the son of man—would all simultaneously be present in Christ. Only when he came did this become clear.

So one might say that features like the sacrifices were meaningful at that stage, and when Christ came, it became clear that they had no value in themselves. But even this view creates the problem that Hebrews states it as *a fact*, not merely as an afterthought: "It is impossible for the blood of bulls and goats to take away sins" (10:4). It does not say that only afterward did it become apparent.

Is it possible that this lack of clarity or a neat answer to the problem reminds us that we do not know or understand everything? This passage in Hebrews may help keep us humble. Some people do not know enough to realize that they have no answer; others know enough to realize this!

SUGGESTED READING

☐   Hebrews 11

☐   Hebrews 12

Reflection

Why do you think Hebrews handles the Old Testament in a different way than Paul does?

_____

_____

_____

_____

In what ways does the author use chapter 11 to encourage the readers of Hebrews?

_____

_____

_____

_____

What do you make of the "prosperity gospel"? What role does suffering play in the Christian life?

_____

_____

_____

_____

What parts of chapter 11 are special to you? Why?

_____

_____

_____

_____

What is the significance of Abraham in the Old Testament? (Compare the portrayal in Hebrews 11 with the one in Galatians 3.)

_____

_____

_____

_____

In comparing Christ with characters in the Old Testament, the author never refers to the prophets (except in Hebrews 1:1, which is no real comparison). Why? I did not deal with this question. I am still myself looking for a reason. Can you think of one?

_____

_____

_____

_____

6

THE SIX WARNINGS: CAN GRACE BE LOST?

A good pastor or friend knows when to encourage us and when to warn us. Hebrews contains both elements, but a characteristic feature of this letter is its strong warnings.

Warnings against What?

The Letter to Hebrews is well known for its famous chapter 6. Virtually a whole library has been written about it. What does not come to the fore clearly enough in this literature is that Hebrews 6 is but one of six warnings, that these six are related, and that working with them as group is indispensable when trying to understand Hebrews 6. The warnings are found in Hebrews 2:1–4; 3:7–4:11; 5:11–6:12; 10:26–39; 12:14–17; and 12:25–29.

Falling from Grace?

In Hebrews, we find the most serious warnings in the entire New Testament. The central question that readers are confronted with is whether believers can fall from grace. In a sense, the entire letter is one cry to believers not to forsake the faith. Let us look at this warning, which dominates all six examples:

- These believers are God's house "if indeed we hold firmly to our confidence and the hope in which we glory" (3:6).

- The believers "have come to share in Christ, if indeed we hold our original conviction firmly to the very end" (3:14). Therefore they should encourage one another daily so that no one has "a sinful, unbelieving heart" (3:12). What is the implication if one does not hold firmly—if one has a sinful, unbelieving heart?

- "Let us be careful that none of you be found to have fallen short" of God's "rest that still stands" (4:1).

- We read about those who "shrink back and are destroyed" (10:39).

These are grave warnings to believers not to fall from grace. The other three warnings sound less sharp, but the point they make is the same:

- Believers should "pay the most careful attention … so that we do not drift away" (2:1).

- "How shall we escape if we ignore so great a salvation?" (2:3).

- "See to it that no one falls short of the grace of God" (12:15).

Isn't this falling from grace? What else can it mean to drift away, to ignore salvation, to fall short of the grace of God?

There are a few interesting examples used to illustrate the warning.

- More than once we read about the Israelites who died in the desert because of their disobedience. These Israelites did not enter the promised land. The readers are warned lest this happens to them, that they may fall short (3:7–4:2). What else could this be than a warning not to fall from grace?

- The example of 6:7–8 moves in the same direction: producing a crop, one receives the blessing of God. The land that produces thorns and thistles is in danger of being cursed.

- Esau, who sold his inheritance, was rejected (12:16–17).

- During the exodus the people "refused him who warned them on earth" and did not escape. "How much less will we?" (12:25). Remember, "God is a consuming fire" (12:29).

Exhortations

These warnings also contain some exhortations. These are positive directives how to avoid the danger.

- The long warning in chapters 3 and 4 ends with the exhortation, "Let us, therefore, make every effort to enter that rest, so that no one will perish by following their [Israel's] example of disobedience" (4:11). Thus here the implication is one of perishing if they do not obey.

- The exhortation in 6:11–12 gives the same impression. The author wants them to persevere to the end. He does "not want [them] to become lazy." Beautiful encouragements, but why? "So that what you hope for may be fully realized." To "inherit what has been promised." Clearly the implication is that they will not inherit if they do not persevere to the end.

- The same point is found in 10:36.

The theme throughout remains the same. Even in the positive exhortations, the implication seems to be that believers can fall from grace.

Hebrews 6

Hebrews 6 has always been in the forefront of this discussion. In addition to a warning about falling from grace, chapter 6 seems to contain a warning that certain sin is unpardonable. We will attend to the "unpardonable sin" in the following chapter.

There are some who try to show that the people spoken of here are not true believers but only apparent ones, people who *seemed* to believe but did not really do so. They build this view on the five things said about these people (Heb 6:4–5).

- They "have once been enlightened."
- They "have tasted the heavenly gift."
- They "have shared in the Holy Spirit."

- They "have tasted the goodness of the word of God."

- They have tasted "the powers of the coming age."

These are all things, it is said, they have *experienced,* things *given* to them, but not things they themselves *did.* It is argued that there is no indication of any initiative taken by them in response to the things given to them.

Immediately after this we have the reasons why they cannot be brought back to repentance. These are things they really did (Heb 6:6):

- They "are crucifying the Son of God all over again."

- They "are subjecting him to public disgrace."

Does this mean that while having *experienced* wonderful things, they *do* only the negative?

It seems that the example that follows moves in the same direction. These people are like land that drinks in the rain (experience) but then "produces thorns and thistles." This land will be burned (6:7–8). Even in this example of the land, the principle is clear: the land has received much but has produced nothing meaningful, so it is to be burned. This seems to imply that these people have experienced the grace of God but have never responded positively. Officially they became part of the community of faith, having experienced the wonderful gifts of God, but they never bore the fruit of conversion. They *seemed* to be Christians but never really were.

Further support for this view can be found in the fact that such a long list of experiences—five—are mentioned.

Why? Why not speak simply of believers as the other five warnings seem to do? Does heaping up the experiences these believers had make the point of how close one may come without really entering the kingdom of God? This is indeed a view to be taken seriously. Is the loss of grace at stake here? Or is it rather an example of how close people can come to Christ without really being born again? Just think of James, who wrote that faith without good works cannot save (Jas 2:14–26). Paul also warned that one can "receive God's grace in vain" (2 Cor 6:1). Can this also be related to John's branch, which can bear no fruit without being attached to the vine and which will be burnt (John 15:6)?

However, this view has to face two serious questions. First is whether the experiences referred to can really be those of a person that has not been saved. Could "the heavenly gift" mean anything less that the grace of God? And why is the fact that they bore no fruit not specifically mentioned but at best only implied? Second, why does it seem clear that all other warnings speak of true Christians who fall from grace?

We may receive more light on chapter 6 in the following chapter when we look at the unpardonable sin. I am still at a loss about what to me seems a tension between the people who seem to be true Christians but the example of the land that is not producing fruit. On the whole these warnings—or at least four of them—seem to be directed at true Christians who may fall from grace. But we will now go deeper into this issue.

Can Believers Fall from Grace?

Through the centuries of Christian theology this has been a burning issue. And besides smaller differences there are two opposing views: a negative one, and a positive one.

Yes

Many Christians and groups of Christians believe that we can fall from grace. The urgent warnings of Hebrews are some of the strongest supports for this view. But there are more.

BIBLICAL SUPPORT: "YES"

In the New Testament, a number of people seem to have lost their faith or to be likely to do so in the future.

☐ Matthew 24:10, 12: In speaking about the future, Jesus sounds the warning that "many will turn away from the faith … and the love of most will grow cold."

☐ 1 Timothy 1:19–20: Here, Paul refers to people who "have suffered shipwreck with regard to the faith."

☐ 1 Timothy 4:1: Here, we read that "in later times some will abandon the faith."

☐ 2 Timothy 2:16–18: Here again, Paul is referring to those "who have departed from the truth" and are destroying the faith of others.

☐ Throughout the New Testament, Old Testament figures or the people themselves who were rejected are referred to in warnings to Christians (Rom 12; 1 Cor 10; Heb 12:16).

Warnings

- In 1 Corinthians 10, Paul warns the church very seriously that by continuing to live in sin they may "fall" (1 Cor 10:12). The examples he uses are chosen from the exodus, when the people were disobedient to God and "fell" and were punished severely. They experienced all the blessings of God (10:1–4), but "God was not pleased with most of them" (10:5).

- In Romans 11, Paul writes about the fall and rejection of Israel (11:11, 15) and the salvation of the gentiles. He writes that the Jews who did not accept Jesus as Messiah were "broken off" like branches from an olive tree (the true people of God). The gentles who believed were "grafted" on to this tree. And then the grave warning to the gentile believers: "If God did not spare the natural branches [the Jews], he will not spare you either" (11:21). God's kindness will continue for them *if* they remain true; "otherwise, you also will be cut off" (11:22).

- Revelation issues serious warnings to the churches—to the same effect. "If you do not repent, I will come to you and remove your lampstand from its place" (2:5). Can a church be destroyed without its members falling from grace? "Because you are lukewarm ... I am about to spit you out of my mouth" (3:16).

- Hebrews, as we have just seen, includes some serious warnings. The Jews that have accepted Christ as the Messiah consider turning their

backs on him and moving back to their Old
Testament-based faith. The writer seems
to warn them that they will thereby lose
their salvation.

The Call to Persevere

In a number of places, believers are called upon to persevere so that in the end they will share in the coming glory.

- Matthew 24:13: "The one who stands firm to the
  end will be saved."

- John 15:1–8: In the metaphor of the true vine,
  Jesus warns that the Father "cuts off every
  branch in me that bears no fruit" (15:2); again,
  "If you do not remain in me, you are like a
  branch that is thrown away and withers; such
  branches are picked up, thrown into the fire and
  burned" (15:6). Hebrews 10:31 comes to mind: "It
  is a dreadful thing to fall into the hands of the
  living God"; again, "for our God is a consuming
  fire" (Heb 12:29).

- In Colossians 1:23, Paul calls upon the church
  members to continue in their faith and not be
  moved from the hope of the gospel.

- In Hebrews, we have already looked at the serious calls on believers to continue in the faith
  (see 3:14; 4:11).

- In Revelation, perseverance is also at stake: "To
  the one who is victorious and does my will to the
  end, I will give authority over the nations" (2:26).

Positive Attitude

However, it is striking how positive New Testament writers can be toward the believers they warn. The classic example is in Hebrews: in 6:4–8, we have what may be the most serious warning against falling from grace. But immediately after the warning the author writes that he is "convinced of better things in your case—the things that have to do with salvation" (6:9), referring to their work and love in helping God's people (6:10). However, even this positive attitude is immediately followed by the wish that they should continue until the end. Even in the positive attitude, a warning is implied.

From this perspective, the New Testament is so clear that nothing more than these lists are necessary to decide the issue: the New Testament clearly describes the possibility that believers can fall from grace. If not, these references simply make no sense. Christians who hold this perspective also believe that the conviction that there is no falling away works negatively on the attitude of believers: they are not serious about being Christians; they are lazy; there is a coolness in their attitude; they lack enthusiasm.

No

This is the opposite position: there is no falling from grace. Once a child of God, always a child of God. Surely believers can backslide, even to the point of seeming to totally lose their faith, but in principle they cannot fall from grace. It has nothing to do with them, with their still somehow remaining true or clinging to God, and has everything to do with God, with his faithfulness. He is true. He will not let go of his children. He will somehow bring them back or hold on to them.

These are as strong about the faithfulness of God as are the warnings of falling from grace. To some, this view is related to very specific views on salvation and election. God has elected specific individuals and will surely save them to the end. This argument concerns the faithfulness

---

BIBLICAL SUPPORT: "NO"

☐   John 10:28–29: "I give them eternal life, and they shall never perish; no one will snatch them out of my hand. My Father, who has given them to me, is greater than all; no one can snatch them out of my Father's hand."

☐   Matthew 24:24: "For false messiahs and false prophets will appear and perform great signs and wonders to deceive, if possible, even the elect." The implication is that this is impossible.

☐   Romans 11:29: "For God's gifts and his call are irrevocable."

☐   Philippians 1:6: "He who began a good work in you will carry it on to completion until the day of Christ Jesus."

☐   Psalm 125:1: "Those who trust in the LORD are like Mount Zion, which cannot be shaken but endures forever."

☐   Isaiah 54:10: "'Though the mountains be shaken and the hills be removed, yet my unfailing love for you will not be shaken nor my covenant of peace be removed,' says the LORD."

of God, and who will ever doubt this? The decisive factor is not what these people do but what God does.

As far as salvation goes, it is not that we repent and God, responding to our initiative, gives us the new birth. It is his initiative. He gives us a new heart, and from this new heart we respond and repent. First regeneration, God's work in us; only then conversion, our response to his initiative. He is faithful and true. He will not let go of the works of his hands (Ps 138:8).

What Now?

We are confronted with one of the most difficult differences between two groups of Christians—both sincere and calling on solid scriptural support. It seems the Yes-group approaches the problem from the human side and the No-group from God's side.

- The Yes-group argues that throughout the New Testament we are called upon to remain true to God and are warned against falling from grace— so in the end it depends on what we do.

- The No-group argues that throughout the Bible we hear of the unfailing faithfulness of God, who takes the initiative in saving us and will not let go of the works of his hands. Our salvation is his work, not ours, and he will keep true to us simply because he is true to himself (2 Tim 2:13). Even our faith is a gift of God (according to a possible translation of Eph 2:8). That is the real reason why believers will not be lost.

- The Yes-group may respond that they will surely
  not denounce the initiative of God in our salvation. As far as God is concerned, no believer will
  ever be lost. Jesus promised exactly this: "no one
  will snatch them out of my hand" (John 10:28).
  But we ourselves can move out of his hand, and
  this has nothing to do with God's initiative or
  faithfulness. It is *our* responsibility to remain
  true to him even as it is *our* responsibility to
  respond and come to him when he calls us
  through the gospel.

- The Yes-group will probably not accept the
  view that it is God who gives us the faith to
  believe and will prefer the common translation
  of Ephesians 2:8. Our salvation is his initiative,
  but *we* have to respond to this initiative. Our
  perseverance again is his initiative, but again we
  have to respond to this. This is how the covenant
  works; it has two sides.

What now? Isn't it true that both views have strong biblical support?

Promise and Faith

The No-group emphasizes God's promises, but the Yes-
group may ask whether they are clear on the fact that his
promises are not merely neutral information from which
anyone can draw logical conclusions. Unbelievers cannot
count on God's promises. Without faith one cannot claim
God's promises. This means that I can only *in faith*—that

is, while trusting in him—accept that no one can "snatch" me out of his hand.

And what then, the Yes-group will ask, of a believer

- who does not stand firm "to the end" (Matt 24:13)?

- who moves "from the hope held out in the gospel" (Col 1:23)?

- who ignores "so great a salvation" (Heb 2:3)?

- who "deliberately [keeps] on sinning" (Heb 10:26)?

If believers cannot fall from grace, what do these warnings mean to such believers?

At least some of the No-group may agree that unfaithful believers should be warned in this way but then hold that because they are elect, they surely will respond positively and repent; if a person never repents, he or she never really was a true believer. But isn't this an opportunistic or facile solution in view of the embarrassing evidence to the contrary?

Is There a Solution?

Would it be acceptable to approach this problem from two different sides?

- From God's side: the faithful are secure. No one can be snatched from his hand.

- From our side: We are seriously warned against falling from grace, and we have to accept these warnings seriously.

Would this mean that we have to respond in two different ways to the situation of two different believers?

- If believers start doubting for whatever reason, or feel uncertain/unable about persevering to the end, I will support and encourage them with the wonderful promise of Jesus: that no one will snatch them from the hand of God, that God will help them overcome temptations (1 Cor 10:13).

- However, if believers seem to start turning their backs on Jesus and are on the brink of denying him, I have to warn them seriously not to play with fire, not to trample the Son of God underfoot, not to insult the Spirit (Heb 10:29), or else they may "fall into the hands of the living God" (10:31).

An Open Situation?

In my view we have to accept this open situation. Let us look at Romans 11 by way of comparison.

Paul and the Gentiles

Paul finds the startling situation that the Roman church is filled with *gentiles* while Jesus is the Messiah of *Israel*. So he asks two questions:

- "Did God reject his people?" (Rom 11:1).

- "Did they stumble so as to fall beyond recovery?" (Rom 11:11).

In both cases his answer is "no":

- Question one: Israel as such has not been rejected, since there is a remnant present in the church (Rom 11:1–6), Paul himself being a Jew. He reminds his readers that also in the Old Testament at times the faithful were few.

- Question two: Israel's fall has not been final. On the contrary, because of their fall, "salvation has come to the Gentiles to make Israel envious" (11:11). Can we say "there is method in madness"?

Paul then makes a very interesting statement concerning his aim as apostle: as the apostle for the gentiles, "I take pride in my ministry *in the hope that I may somehow arouse my own people to envy and save some of them*" (Rom 11:13–14, emphasis mine). Then he tries to tell us how he understands this abnormal situation of *gentiles* filling the church while they follow the Messiah of the *Jews*.

The Olive Tree

He uses the olive tree as illustration. The true Israel of the Old Testament is the natural olive. But when the Messiah came, the people rejected him. Toward the end of his ministry Jesus warned the leaders, "Therefore I tell you that the kingdom of God will be taken away from you and given to a people that will produce its fruit" (Matt 21:43). Again: "Look, your house is left to you desolate" (Matt 23:38). This means that the Israel that has rejected Jesus is rejected by God. That is what Paul refers to as the branches of the natural olive that are broken off (Rom 11:17).

In the meantime gentiles accepted Jesus. They are the branches of the wild olive that have been "grafted in" on the natural olive tree (Rom 11:17). This, then, is the situation in Paul's day: Jews are rejected, and gentiles fill the church. But is it final?

No. Remember, Paul started with two statements: God did not reject his people, and they did not fall beyond recovery (Rom 11:1, 11). Therefore he continues: "And if they [the Jews who have rejected Jesus] do not persist in unbelief, they will be grafted in, for God is able to graft them in again" (Rom 11:23). This means that to unbelieving Israel the door of salvation is still open. Paul indeed was working for exactly that—their return, when they will accept Jesus as Messiah.

And what of the gentiles? They have come in; they were grafted onto the natural olive tree. But they get the warning: "Do not be arrogant, but tremble. For if God did not spare the natural branches, he will not spare you either" (Rom 11:20–21). If they will not continue in God's kindness, they also will be cut off (Rom 11:22). This means that the "back door" remains open to the gentiles. They can be cut off as Israel has been if they do not continue in the faith. The rejected Israel can come in again, and the accepted gentiles can be cut off.

None of us enjoy receiving warnings! However, a moment's reflection will alert us to how important they can be. We need to know that we will be burned if we get too close to fire; we do want to be warned if there are sharks in water into which we are going for a swim. In Hebrews the warnings are not only important, but they also alert us to how much is at stake in our relationship to Christ. It is a matter of life and death.

SUGGESTED READING

Read carefully again through the six warnings:

☐ Hebrews 2:1–4

☐ Hebrews 3:7–4:11

☐ Hebrews 5:11–6:12

☐ Hebrews 10:26–39

☐ Hebrews 12:14–17

☐ Hebrews 12:25–29

Reflection

What do you think—can believers fall from grace? Why or why not?

_____

_____

_____

_____

Who are the people of Hebrews 6: believers, or mere apparent believers?

_____

_____

_____

_____

Is the open situation of Romans 11 applicable to individuals or only to groups like Israel and the gentiles?

_____

_____

_____

_____

Why is the author of Hebrews positive about the possibility that the people of Hebrews 6 will indeed be saved?

_____

_____

_____

_____

How would you encourage a Christian who has lost interest in the faith, in light of the passages in this chapter?

_____

_____

_____

_____

7

THE UNFORGIVABLE SIN

Its Occurrence in the New Testament

In this regard Hebrews has always attracted attention. It is more than the possibility of falling from grace (see chapter 6). It is about the question whether there is a sin that excludes someone from grace, that makes it impossible to return. Hebrews has at least three references which may be the strongest in the entire New Testament: 6:4–6; 10:26–27; and 12:14–17.

6:4–6

According to these verses it is impossible for those who have committed this sin—"who have once been enlightened ... and who have fallen away"—to be brought back to repentance.

10:26–27

According to these verses there is no sacrifice left for those who "deliberately keep on sinning after [they] have received the knowledge of the truth." What remains for them is "only a fearful expectation of judgment and of raging fire that will consume the enemies of God."

12:14-17

These verses seem to move in the same direction. It starts with four exhortations:

- They should do everything possible to live in peace with everyone and to be holy.

- They should not fall short of the grace of God.

- No bitter roots should grow up in them.

- They should not be sexually immoral and godless.

The example of Esau is used. He sold his inheritance rights as the firstborn. When, afterward, he wanted to inherit this blessing, he was rejected, even though he sought the blessing with tears. This implies that there was no turning back.

Thus in these warnings there is no way back, no possible repentance, no sacrifice for this sin. It seems this sin excludes one from grace. It seems one oversteps a boundary from which there is no return. What is this all about? What sin is this?

This is an urgent question. It seems contrary to the great message of the Bible about the abundance of God's grace and his boundless forgiveness. We read "that God was reconciling the world to himself in Christ, not counting people's sins against them" (2 Cor 5:19). And again, Christ "is the atoning sacrifice for our sins, and

not only for ours but also for the sins of the whole world"
(1 John 2:2).

On the other hand these words about an unforgivable
sin are not limited to Hebrews. We also find them in the
Gospels and in 1 John. Jesus said: "And so I tell you, every
kind of sin and slander can be forgiven, but blasphemy
against the Spirit will not be forgiven" (Matt 12:31; see also
Mark 3:28, 29; Luke 12:10.) In 1 John 5:16–17, we read: "If
you see any brother or sister commit a sin that does not
lead to death, you should pray and God will give them life.
... There is a sin that leads to death. I am not saying that
you should pray about that."

In the Gospels this sin is called the sin against the
Holy Spirit, and there we also have a clear distinction
between this sin against the Spirit and sin against Jesus.
A word against the Son of Man will be forgiven, but not
one against the Spirit, "either in this age or in the age to
come" (Matt 12:32). We are left with two questions:

- What is this sin, and why can it not be forgiven?

- Why this distinction between the Son and
  the Spirit?

What Is It?

Let us first look at the Gospels. The context of this
saying of Jesus in Matthew 12 is important. Jesus healed
a demon-possessed man. The people were astonished. The
Pharisees, clearly alarmed by the enthusiasm of the crowd,
tried to counter this by accusing Jesus of doing this by the
power of Beelzebul, "the prince of demons" (Matt 12:24).
But Jesus responded by showing the ridiculousness and

malice of their accusation, that Satan drives out Satan, and continued: "But if it is by the Spirit of God that I drive out demons, then the kingdom of God has come upon you" (Matt 12:28; see also Luke 11:20). The urgent warning of blasphemy against the Spirit follows. Why? Because the Pharisees maliciously try to refute the irrefutable, to deny the undeniable and indisputable with a fallacy. They see the facts clearly in front of them—a miracle destroying the power of evil—but they attribute it deliberately to Satan. Thus it seems that this sin is the intentional distortion of the obvious fact of the work of the Holy Spirit.

In Hebrews it seems that we have more or less the same depiction of this sin. People deliberately keep on sinning after they have received the knowledge of truth (Heb 10:26).

Why the Distinction between Jesus and the Spirit?

Why can sin against the Son of Man be forgiven, but not sin against the Holy Spirit (Matt 12:32)? In Hebrews, this distinction disappears: the sin is against the Spirit *and* Jesus. Those sin "who [have] trampled the Son of God underfoot ... and who [have] insulted the Spirit of grace" (Heb 10:29). In Hebrews 6:6, *only* Christ is mentioned! Why is Christ now on equal footing with the Spirit? Or rather, why were they not on the same footing in the Gospels?

Is it because the situation was still quite different during Jesus' life on earth? Is it that Jesus was still the humiliated one, the one about whom even the disciples themselves were in doubt? Is it because the real meaning of Jesus was still uncertain, that even the disciples misunderstood him again and again (Mark 8:32–33; 9:32; 10:35–37)? Is it that even Jesus himself still tried to hide his messiahship to the people (Matt 16:20)? So he could still be misunderstood, rejected, and even scolded (Luke 7:33–35)?

But after that he was crucified and raised to glory. At that stage the uncertainty was gone. Those who "have received the knowledge of the truth" (Heb 10:26) now knew he was the Son of God, equal to the Father. So at this stage the difference was erased, and the unpardonable sin is as much sin against him as against the Spirit.

Why Is This Sin Unforgivable?

In Hebrews 6:6 a reason is given: "To their loss they are crucifying the Son of God all over again and subjecting him to public disgrace." The cross had been to the advantage of all, but this time it is to the loss, the disadvantage of these people. Why can this sin not be forgiven? The first time Christ even explicitly forgave those who were crucifying him (Luke 23:34). Is it again because the situation has radically changed, as we have seen just now? He is no longer the humiliated, mocked Jew; he is the triumphant Son of God, raised to glory, and these people know it, they have experienced him (6:4). They "have received the knowledge of the truth" (10:26).

Have another look at chapter 6. They crucify him "all over again." Does it mean that they confirm his first crucifixion, that they support the religious leaders' judgment that he has blasphemed God, that he had to die because of his own sin? And isn't this the meaning of Hebrews 10:26, that "no sacrifice for sins is left," since they reject the one and only sacrifice acceptable to God for the sins of the world: the cross of Jesus? So they exclude themselves from the grace of God? Is this the reason why this sin cannot be forgiven?

In the Gospels the unpardonable sin is sin against the Spirit. Now, in Hebrews, the letter on the magnificence of Christ, the sin is said to be sin against Christ. Losing him is losing everything. How wonderfully this fits the overall message of Hebrews, the letter to the Christians who hesitated in following Christ.

Again, looking back to Hebrews 6:4, readers should see at least two ways of handling these most difficult words. The main sentence runs: "It is impossible for those ... to be brought back to repentance." One interpretation runs that it is impossible merely for humans, but surely not for God, for whom everything is possible. This is a forced interpretation, not taking into account that "impossible" clearly has a general meaning here. The other interpretation is to accept that it is impossible for others to bring this man back to repentance, but that he himself can come back. This does not take the overall meaning into account nor the meaning of the other five warnings.

But we have now been dealing only with Hebrews, not with the Gospels. In Hebrews it seems the reason is that these people reject Christ himself and the meaning of the cross. Without him and his cross, it is impossible to be saved. The Gospels refer to the Pharisees maliciously trying to refute the irrefutable, to deny the undeniable and indisputable with a fallacy. Thus it seems that this sin is the intentional distortion of the obvious facts to deny the work of the Holy Spirit.

THE HISTORICAL TRUSTWORTHINESS OF THE GOSPELS

It may seem strange now to look at the trustworthiness of the Gospels while we are working on Hebrews. But let us nevertheless try something in the light of the issue we have been dealing with: the difference between the Gospels and Hebrews in terms of the unpardonable sin. According to the Gospels, sin against Christ can be forgiven, but not sin against the Spirit. But according to Hebrews, sin against neither of the two can be forgiven. Why the difference? Our answer is that there is a huge difference between the humiliated and mocked Jesus in the Gospels and the raised and glorified Christ in Hebrews.

The Gospels are not diaries, brought up to date every evening after the experiences of the day. They were written some 30 years or more after the cross and resurrection of Christ. By the time Matthew wrote his Gospel, Christ had been glorified decades back. By the time Matthew wrote, everyone knew that Christ was on the same footing as the Spirit. But he still writes that Jesus said sin against him can be forgiven, only sin against the Spirit cannot. What significance does this have? It shows us that Matthew carefully wrote what had happened and was said three decades earlier, even though in the meantime the perspective had changed radically and everyone knew it. This helps us in our response to theologians who disclaim the historical trustworthiness of the Gospels and claim that each writer simply "painted" the picture of Jesus he preferred or needed and that we can do the same ourselves.

Is this really different from Hebrews? Isn't the main difference that while in the Gospels it is sin against the Spirit, in Hebrews it is mainly against Christ (but of course also against the Spirit)? What is the difference between radically rejecting the cross of Jesus and as radically rejecting the work of the Spirit? Can we reject the work of the Spirit but still cling to the cross? After all is said and done, we still end with a question. Our position is that it is impossible to be saved without the cross of Christ and the work of the Spirit. But why can't the person come back?

Jesus did not answer this question in the Gospels. In Hebrews the answer seems to be because they reject and again crucify Christ. But why can't they repent from having done this? I find no clear answer in Hebrews nor elsewhere in the Bible. So I just take the warning as it stands.

SUGGESTED READING

- ☐   Hebrews 6:4–6
- ☐   Hebrews 10:26–27
- ☐   Hebrews 12:14–17

Reflection

How do you understand the unforgivable sin? How is it related to our main theme of the magnificence of Christ?

_____

_____

_____

_____

What has struck you most in your study of Hebrews?

_____

_____

_____

_____

What new things have you learned? How will they change the way you live?

_____

_____

_____

_____

Have you ever come across the view that the Gospels are not historically trustworthy and that every writer simply created a picture of Jesus in terms of his own preferences? How did you (or would you) respond?

_____

_____

_____

_____

At the end of the day, it is all about Christ. Take time to reflect on how he is depicted in Hebrews and respond to him.

_____

_____

_____

_____

CONCLUSION

Although often neglected, in my view the Letter to the Hebrews is comparable only to Paul's Letter to the Romans in the New Testament in terms of its focus on Christ and its unpacking of all that God has done for us in Christ. Intriguingly, Paul and the author of Hebrews unpack events in significantly different ways, drawing on different vocabulary and concepts. This is not to suggest for a moment that they contradict each other, but it is to say that so huge an event as Christ's life is like a multifaceted diamond, which can be viewed from different angles.

The focus of Hebrews is Christ, and my hope is that as you work through and reflect upon this letter, you will find yourselves again and again emerging in his magnificent presence, encouraged to persevere in following him.

RESOURCES FOR FURTHER STUDY

Attridge, Harold. *Hebrews*. Hermeneia. Minneapolis: Fortress, 1989.

Cockerill, Gareth L. *The Epistle to the Hebrews*. NICNT. Grand Rapids: Eerdmans, 2012.

Ellingforth, Paul. *The Epistle to the Hebrews*. NIGTC. Grand Rapids: Eerdmans, 1993.

Jobes, Karen H. *Letters to the Church: A Survey of Hebrews and the General Epistles*. Grand Rapids: Zondervan, 2011.

Lane, William L. *Hebrews 1–8*. WBC 47A. Grand Rapids: Zondervan, 1991.

———. *Hebrews 9–13*. WBC 47B. Grand Rapids: Zondervan, 1991.

NOTES

1. See Gareth L. Cockerill, *The Epistle to the Hebrews*, NICNT (Grand Rapids: Eerdmans, 2012), 2–10.

2. Cockerill, *Hebrews*, 41.

3. Cockerill, *Hebrews*, 9.

4. This is a modified version of Paul Ellingworth's outline in *The Epistle to the Hebrews*, NIGTC (Grand Rapids: Eerdmans, 1993).

5. Cf. Cockerill, *Hebrews*, 16–23.

6. Paul Ellingworth, "The Old Testament in Hebrews: Exegesis, Method and Hermeneutics." Diss., University of Aberdeen, 1977. See the very useful article by George H. Guthrie, "Hebrews' Use of the Old Testament: Recent Trends in Research," *CBR* 1.2 (2003): 271–94.

7. William L. Lane, *Hebrews 1–8*. WBC 47A. (Grand Rapids: Zondervan, 1991), cxvi.

8. B. F. Westcott, *The Epistle to the Hebrews*, (Grand Rapids: Eerdmans, 1950), 475.

9. Hebrews quotes Psalms more often than any other New Testament book. The next closest is Romans. See the diagram in Gert J. Steyn, *A Quest for the Assumed LXX Vorlage of the Explicit Quotations in Hebrews* (Göttingen: Vandenhoeck and Ruprecht, 2011), 12.

10. On the use of Habakkuk 2:3–4 LXX in Hebrews 10, see Gheorghita, *The Role of the Septuagint in Hebrews*, 147–224.

11. J. Walters, "The Rhetorical Arrangement of Hebrews," unpublished paper. See Lane, *Hebrews 1–8*, cxiv–cxv.

12. George B. Caird, "The Exegetical Method of the Epistle to the Hebrews," *CJT* 5 (1959): 44–51. Cf. Guthrie, "Hebrews," 920.

13. See Richard Longenecker, *Biblical Exegesis in the Apostolic Period* (Grand Rapids: Eerdmans, 1999), 175.

14. Isaac Watts, "Joy to the World" (1719).